Tweets and Hurricanes

by Sandy Stream
Illustrated by Yoko Matsuoka

Tweets and Hurricanes. By Sandy Stream
Illustrated by Yoko Matsuoka
Edited by Tomoko Matsuoka

ISBN 978-0-9739481-4-1

Copyright © 2014 by Sandy Stream Publishing. Montreal, Canada.
All rights reserved. No part of this book may be reproduced, stored in a retrieval system, or transmitted in any form or by any means without the written permission of Sandy Stream Publishing.

On a Personal Note

What happens after an ordeal is over? If it is actually over, why do our bodies still feel it and not move on? When one thing ends, it is often just the beginning...

This book is intended to help you see how your body can still be carrying and living in the past.

We do, however, have a built-in ability to heal. To access this ability, one must learn to stop judging the body and stop judging what it needs to heal. In other words, you must do what is the easiest and most difficult thing for humans to do. Just allow. Simply let the body complete its cycle without interfering with it through your judgmental mind.

Even if something appears frozen, the life force that is transmitted by simple observation gives it the spark needed to move and liberate itself. It is only then that your body can be in the "now."

Sandy Stream

Based on *many*
true stories

Sparky and his mama were together again.

River was happy but worried. The sparkle in Sparky's eyes was not quite the same as it used to be before he was taken by the giant.

So River flew to the edge of the forest to find the wise owl to ask how she could help Sparky.

The wise owl turned to River and said, "Go to the cave and you will see that the answer is in you."

Mama went to the cave. She looked around. There was nothing but bare cave walls and a little river that ran by the side of the cave.

She thought and thought and thought.

Then she understood!
The answer was inside her—River—
in the river!
She understood that the river
was water, and that Sparky
needed to cry.

She brought Sparky to the river and watched him cry for thirty days and thirty nights. He cried for all the times no one came to help him.

All the tweets he held inside came out and flooded the river.

Mama let him cry until every single tweet in his throat came out. She let him tweet any words and sounds that were held in. She let him tweet his upset at her for not helping him, and she even let him cry that he missed the giant in some way...

...because that is what he felt.

And then he was better. All the tweets were out and the sparkle in his eyes came back. Mama hugged Sparky and he flew away to play.

River now looked at her own body and at her weak eyes. She went to the cave every day and cried like Sparky had.

It helped a bit...but not enough.

She went to the wise owl again to ask for help.
The wise owl just repeated the same words, "The answer is in you."

River did not understand.
She looked at the river over and over.
She watched how it flowed. But she did not get better.

One winter day, the squawks in River's throat grew so big that she could hardly eat or swallow.

She went to the wise owl again, who said: "Your old squawks are stuck in your throat; just let them out naturally like a river."

Mama sat near the river.
She let out her squawks—the ones she had held in for so long. Her squawks were so loud that the cave shook.

"LEAVE HIM ALONE!" "DON'T TAKE SPARKY!" "DON'T TAKE HIM!" "SPARKY, BE CAREFUL!" "GET OUT, ESCAPE! OPEN THE CAGE!" "FLY, SPARKY, FLY!"

...and she was able to eat again.

But she still could not fly well…
Her body had so much turmoil inside—like a hurricane of strong winds and waves.
She went to see the wise owl again.

The wise owl told her:
"Go sit in front of the river for thirty days and come back to see me."
So River sat in front of the river for thirty days and thirty nights, trying to calm the hurricane inside.

But nothing happened. She could not calm herself. She went back to the wise owl and said, "I was not able to calm down my hurricane. I tried but I couldn't."

The wise owl said:
"Who told you to try anything?
Does a river try? Who told you to calm yourself down? Does a river calm itself down? Just be like water."
River understood.

She went back to the cave and sat near the river. She lay down and closed her eyes.
She trembled and sent ripples into the water.
She trembled for as long as her body wanted.
She let her body be like water.

And then she knew...

She knew that she had to let out the hurricane that raged inside. She knew that she could only be back to herself after the hurricane was released.
But she was afraid. She wanted to be a nice bird—she didn't want to be a hurricane.

Be like water... the owl's voice echoed.
The river is not judged, it just is.
A mother also "just is."

River knew it was time to let her body do what it needed to do. She was ready to be like water.

Alone in the cave, she closed her eyes and began seeing Sparky helpless and afraid. She remembered how she could not do anything at all, how she was frozen, frozen, frozen... She did not want to be frozen anymore.

I want to get rid of this hurricane!!
How do I get rid of this hurricane?!

The answer is in you. Be like water. She kept hearing in her head.

It's in the river... A river always moves! It doesn't stop! I HAVE TO MOVE!

River knew what to do.
I will move... I will no longer hold in the hurricane... no matter what it looks like.

She sat, closed her eyes, and started remembering and feeling everything again...
Boom, boom, boom.
Her heart was beating fast.
She watched Sparky being taken, held, yelled at, caressed, frozen, unable to move...

BOOM! BOOM! BOOM!!

River felt the hurricane building inside. She would no longer hold it back... She was ready to let it out, here, in the cave, no matter what it looked like.

She felt the hurricane coming. She stood up, closed her eyes, and felt the energy grow inside her, and she let it grow and grow...

BOOM, BOOM, BOOM!

She stretched out her wings and imagined herself being a great white eagle, flying around the cave, causing huge winds. She imagined breaking the window of the castle, rescuing Sparky, and throwing lightning bolts at the giant.

Water splashed everywhere from the river. The storm raged on with wind and rain blowing in every direction... She let out her hurricane over and over and over until it settled.

The river near the cave continued to flow naturally. And now... so did River.

Her muscles settled inside her body. She took a deep breath. It flowed into her claws and her back, softening them.

Tears of relief wet and cleansed her eyes so she could see clearly again...so she could once again see the sparkle in Sparky's eyes.

The now

The River Series

Sparky Can Fly
Sparky's Mama
Tweets and Hurricanes
Feathers
Flex
Roots
The River

www.RiverSpeaks.com

www.ingramcontent.com/pod-product-compliance
Lightning Source LLC
Chambersburg PA
CBHW061121010526
44112CB00024B/2937